Revolutionizing Real Estate

How Blockchain Transforms Property Management

Table of Contents

Chapter 1. Introduction

In this special report, we delve deep into one of the most revolutionary technologies of our time, blockchain, and its burgeoning impact on real estate - a sector that has traditionally been resistant to change. Yet, despite the technical nature of blockchain, you don't need to be a tech guru to understand the transformative power it brings. With an easy-to-understand approach, this comprehensive report shines a light on how blockchain is simplifying property management while increasing efficiency, lowering costs, and opening doors to new investment opportunities. So, whether you're a seasoned property magnate, an innovative startup, or someone intrigued by the entanglement of technology and real estate, this report is a treasure trove of insights that will help you stay ahead of the curve. Take a step into the fascinating world of blockchain-powered real estate and experience for yourself the future of property management!

Chapter 2. Understanding Blockchain: A Simplified Overview

The blockchain is a type of Distributed Ledger Technology (DLT) that gained worldwide recognition due to the advent of cryptocurrencies, in particular, Bitcoin. However, its potential extends far beyond digital currencies, posing a range of benefits for various industries - including real estate.

2.1. What is Blockchain?

In the simplest of terms, a blockchain is a type of database. However, what differentiates it from a classical database is its structure and the ways transactions are stored and organized. Each unit of data in a blockchain—commonly referred to as a block—holds a batch of individual transactions. These blocks are interconnected in a linear, sequential order forming a chain, hence the term 'blockchain.'

Within these transactions, is coded information: who is participating, the details of the transaction, a unique identifier called a 'hash,' and the hash of the previous block in the chain. This last factor is particularly crucial because it makes tampering with the information extraordinarily challenging since the hash of every subsequent block would need to be altered as well.

Blockchain transactions are based on consensus mechanisms. The nodes—in a decentralized network that is blockchain—must agree on the verification of these transactions. Once the majority of nodes reach consensus, the transaction is added to the block.

These are the endearing qualities which make a blockchain secure by design: the blocks' immutability and the decentralized consensus mechanisms. The whole framework is designed to withstand changes made to the data once it's been added to the chain.

2.2. Different Types of Blockchains

Blockchains can be categorized into three distinct types: public, private, and consortium blockchains. Understanding the differences between these types is crucial to realizing the potential applications in the real estate industry.

- **Public Blockchains**: They are open to anyone to participate, validate transactions, and create new blocks. Bitcoin and Ethereum are prime examples of public blockchains. Despite being highly secure and tamper-resistant, they are slower and more energy-consuming than their counterparts.

- **Private Blockchains**: Unlike public blockchains, their access is limited to a specific number of trusted participants. This makes them faster and more efficient, but at the cost of decentralization.

- **Consortium Blockchains**: They are a hybrid of the above two types. Here, multiple organizations control the consensus process, making these blockchains efficient and, at the same time, less prone to centralization.

2.3. Blockchain and Smart Contracts

One technology working hand-in-hand with blockchain is called 'smart contracts.' These are self-executing contracts with the terms of agreement directly written into code. In simpler terms, they automate processes when predefined conditions are met.

For instance, imagine a rental agreement as a smart contract. It could be programmed in a way that initiates a monthly transfer from the tenant to the landlord without needing a middleman. This example gives a taste of how smart contracts can make real estate transactions and property management more efficient.

2.4. Blockchain in Real Estate: An Early Glimpse

Now, understanding these basics of blockchain, when applied to real estate, hints at revolutionary changes. A traditionally paperwork-heavy process becomes streamlined, automated, and significantly more transparent. From property registrations to transactions and leasing processes, blockchain stands to simplify and secure each step.

But that barely scratches the surface. There are numerous potential applications of blockchain in real estate, and we will delve into them in subsequent sections. But one thing is clear from the onset: Just as the internet transformed information flow over the past few decades, blockchain technology promises the same for transactions and contracts in industries like real estate over the next few.

Chapter 3. The Intersection of Real Estate and Blockchain Technology

Innovation has always been a driving force propelling society forward. The introduction of blockchain technology is nothing short of a revolution, creating seismic shifts in financial transactions, data security, and transparency. However, its impact does not stop at the borders of finance. Blockchain has quietly wriggled its way into the real estate sector, promising to address age-old challenges and breathe new life into property management practices.

3.1. The Advent of Blockchain Technology

The advent of blockchain technology was an epochal event. Initially devised for Bitcoin, a cryptocurrency, it has since cast a much larger shadow. It finds its value in allowing digital information to be distributed, but not copied, ensuring a level of security previously unseen.

At the core of blockchain architecture are the basic principles of decentralization, transparency, and immutability. These interplay to provide an infrastructure where peer-to-peer transactions occur in a secure, immutable, and transparent manner overtime. Such characteristics make blockchain particularly appealing to areas where accuracy, authenticity, and trust are paramount, opening up manifold possibilities in truly transformational ways, one of which is real estate.

3.2. Blockchain and Real Estate: A Perfect Union

Though the domain of real estate has been slow to adapt to changes, the influence of blockchain technology has started to percolate through its pores, and for good reason. Real estate, a sector known for its intense reliance on record-keeping, documentation, and transactions, seems primed to benefit from an incorruptible digital ledger.

Blockchain stands to alter the real estate landscape significantly by simplifying processes, increasing accountability, reducing fraud, fostering transparency, and ultimately creating a more efficient and less costly means of managing real estate transactions. Here's how:

3.3. Blockchain in Property Transactions

The conventional process of buying and selling properties is tedious, time-consuming, and often governed by intermediaries, leading to increased costs. Blockchain, thanks to smart contracts, promises to overhaul this. Smart contracts are self-executing contracts programmed to carry out an agreement once specific conditions are met.

With smart contracts, typical property transactions can become straightforward and speedy. The transfer of ownership can be executed instantly once the contract's stipulations are fulfilled, thereby eliminating the lengthy validation process and the need for middlemen. Beyond transaction speed, smart contracts can contribute to reduced transaction costs by shedding superfluous administrative and legal fees.

3.4. Enhanced Transparency

Blockchain's capacity to instill transparency is remarkable, particularly in markets known for opacity like real estate. Property ownership and history details, when encoded on a blockchain, forms an unalterable chain of records. Not only can such publicly accessible, trustworthy data reduce unlawful activities like fraud, but it can also considerably streamline due diligence processes. Buyers can, with confidence, trace the lineage of a property and verify the legitimacy of the sellers, effectively demystifying the real estate transaction process.

3.5. Fractional Ownership and Tokenization

A rather exciting prospect that blockchain brings to the table is fractional ownership via tokenization. Tokenization refers to the process of converting the ownership of an asset into a digital token on a blockchain. This means a property worth a substantial amount can be split into smaller, affordable units, enabling fractional ownership.

Tokenization has the potential to democratize the real estate investment industry. Without the need for high brokerage fees and the ability to invest in portions of expensive properties, a wider range of investors can now partake in real estate investments. Concurrently, it allows property owners to liquidate assets easily, thereby injecting liquidity into an industry known for its insusceptible nature.

3.6. Blockchain's Impact on Property Management

Blockchain can also transform property management by offering robust solutions for recording, tracking, and transferring real estate assets. Implementation of blockchain opens the door to improved record management with its decentralized and immutable database. Details of leases, payments, and maintenance can be stored securely on the platform, enabling easy retrieval and significantly lowering the risk of disputes.

3.7. Conclusion: Charting the Future of Real Estate

The incorporation of blockchain technology into real estate is in its early stages, and the potential for growth is monumental. As adoption becomes more widespread, we can expect a more integrated, seamless, secure, and transparent environment. Blockchain technology is slated to drive the next big evolution in real estate, making it more accessible, efficient, and open than ever before.

Numerous challenges lie ahead, including regulatory uncertainties, integration difficulties, and adoption hurdles. However, the potential benefits that blockchain offers are undeniable and stand to revolutionize real estate markets on a global scale.

In the face of this innovation, real estate industry professionals and interested parties would do well to understand, adapt, and prepare for this emerging technology trend, or risk falling behind in the ever-evolving real estate landscape. The future of real estate is on the blockchain horizon, promising a distinctly transformed sector where technology and property intertwine seamlessly.

Chapter 4. Revamping Property Management With Blockchain

Innovation has become synonymous with survival in the rapidly evolving world of industries. Amongst the emerging technologies spearheading this initiative, blockchain has proven to be one of the most compelling. The digital public ledger is evolving beyond its cryptocurrency roots to permeate various sectors, including real estate, revolutionizing how we manage property today.

4.1. The Basics of Blockchain

Firstly, it is crucial to comprehend the foundational aspect of blockchain technology. As a decentralized digital ledger, it records transactions across many computers, ensuring that the record cannot be altered retroactively without the alteration of all subsequent blocks. The transactions are time-stamped, fostering transparency and removing the need for intermediaries.

Every party has access to the same information, eliminating the need for conventional trust-building measures. No individual can manipulate the data single-handedly, which fosters a trustless environment conducive to business.

4.2. Blockchain and Real Estate

Now that we've established the essential characteristics of blockchain let's delve into its applications in the property market. Here are some aspects to consider:

Property Transactions: Blockchain's trustless environment can significantly speed up and simplify the complex process of buying and selling property. Buyers and sellers can interact directly, decreasing the need for slow and expensive intermediaries like agents, solicitors, and banks.

Facilitating Fractional Ownership: Among the most intriguing aspects of blockchain is its ability to facilitate fractional ownership. Real estate properties could be tokenized, or divided into digital assets, representing a share of the property. This system could democratize property investment, allowing even those with modest capitals to get involved.

Streamline Payments: Blockchain-based payment systems can speed up transactions, reduce fees, and simplify the acquisition of property, especially across borders. It's particularly appealing for dealing with sizable transactions like property sales, and robust security measures minimize the risk of fraud.

4.3. Real-World Applications in Property Management

Having examined the abstract potential of blockchain, let's explore some real-world examples of how this technology is being applied in property management.

Smart Contracts: These are pre-written computer programs that are stored and replicated on the blockchain. They can self-execute when certain conditions are met, greatly simplifying various real estate processes, including lease agreements, property sales, and even dispute resolution processes. Various platforms already employ smart contracts.

Rental and Lease Management: The rental market can greatly benefit from blockchain's transparency. It can help clear ambiguities on who is renting what, for how long, and at what price. Blockchain also allows for digital identities, making it easier to conduct background checks on potential tenants.

Building Management: Blockchain could aid in obtaining permits, registering property, and following official rules and regulations. Decentralizing this process could prove useful in areas like building maintenance and tenant management.

4.4. Challenges and Opportunities

Despite its promise, blockchain is not a cure-all to the sector's challenges. Transaction speeds on the blockchain are greatly dependant on the network's size and could be sluggish in peak times. Also, it is vital to balance transparency with privacy, an area where blockchain protocols are still improving.

Nevertheless, the opportunities are undeniable. More efficient, transparent, and democratic property management is within reach, and the possibility of unlocking new real estate markets makes this an exciting time for all players – from longstanding property magnates to innovative startups.

In conclusion, blockchain technology poses a sea change for property management. With various applications in the pipeline, it is fast becoming an indispensable tool. However, like any innovation, it comes with challenges that need to be acknowledged and overcome. By doing so, we inch closer to a future where blockchain is routine in property management, paving a more streamlined and transparent path to real estate success.

Chapter 5. Lowering Costs and Increasing Efficiency in Real Estate Transactions

"Blockchain, with its potential to remove intermediaries, streamline procedures, and increase transparency, stands as a transformative advancement that could significantly circumvent the traditionally high costs and inefficiencies prevalent in the real estate sector. Let's delve into the granular details of how blockchain can lower costs and enhance productivity in real estate transactions.

5.1. Decentralization and Disintermediation

In its design, blockchain boasts an inherent decentralization feature that challenges conventions in essential ways. Traditionally, property transactions have been centralized. A single central authority such as a government land-department holds the official records. Multiple intermediaries (lawyers, brokers, and banks) facilitate transactions, creating a cumbersome, time-consuming, and costly process. Blockchain's decentralized nature implies that no singular entity holds ownership over the information—rather, it is distributed across a network of nodes, each having a copy of the entire blockchain.

This decentralization fosters disintermediation, or the elimination of middlemen, which can significantly lower the costs associated with real estate transactions. For example, by employing smart contracts based on blockchain, much of the work done by lawyers and escrow companies during a transaction—like ensuring terms of the contract are met before the property and money change hands—can be automated. Therefore, the excessive fees charged by these intermediaries could be bypassed.

5.2. Streamlined Due Diligence

For any real estate purchase, due diligence is an essential yet often time-consuming exercise. It necessitates scrutinizing various documents: leases, loans, contracts, and so forth, which often requires hours of legal assistance. Blockchain technology has the potential to simplify this exercise substantially. With a decentralized, unalterable blockchain registry, stakeholders can independently verify property details such as ownership history, legal status and outstanding obligations—substantially reducing the time spent, and hence the expenses incurred, in these activities.

5.3. Transparent and Reduced-cost Property Management

Blockchain also offers increased transparency, another key efficiency. In conventional real estate management, due to partial and selected transparency, property owners often encounter issues ranging from hidden fees to manipulative pricing.

With blockchain, every transaction and contract is recorded and available to everyone on that particular network. This capability, combined with the immutability of blockchain records, promotes transparency and discourages fraudulent activities, greatly reducing costs.

Rental property managements can also benefit considerably from blockchain. As an example, integrating Internet of Things (IoT) devices, such as smart locks, with blockchain technology, can simplify the process of renting. By pairing smart contracts with these devices, property access can be automatically granted to a tenant once they fulfill the payment obligations, disintermediating the need for a manual key exchange process thereby reducing management costs.

5.4. Efficient Cross-Border Transactions

The implicit international aspect of blockchain could make cross-border property transactions smoother and less expensive. Currently, these transactions can be time-consuming and costly due to differences in regulations, currency exchange rate fluctuations and intermediary charges. In fact, currency exchange alone can account for up to 7.5% of the transaction costs. Blockchain, by facilitating direct peer-to-peer foreign transactions, has the potential to eliminate these problems by making property investment and funding increasingly borderless, thereby reducing both time and costs substantially.

5.5. Accelerating Real Estate Liquidity

Finally, blockchain introduces the prospect of tokenizing real estate assets—making them tradeable like stocks or commodities. This feature converts illiquid assets into liquid ones, increasing market efficiency and reducing the need for costly brokerages or listing services. Through this, even smaller investors can partake in real estate investments which were otherwise only in the reach of investors with considerable capital.

It can be stated without contention that blockchain has the capacity to revolutionize real estate transactions by downsizing cost-intensive processes, eliminating the need for intermediaries, and enhancing transparency. While it's bear in mind that harnessing the full potential of blockchain is still a vision of the future, these blockchain-powered breakthroughs are progressively making their way into the industry, laying a blueprint for a more cost-effective and efficient real estate sector."

Chapter 6. Unlocking New Investment Opportunities in Real Estate

The inception of blockchain has paved the way for an entire generation of new investment opportunities in real estate. While initially perceived as an enabling technology for cryptocurrencies such as Bitcoin, blockchain's potential for creating a more transparent, efficient, and democratic real estate sector is rapidly becoming apparent.

6.1. The Paradigm Shift to Blockchain-Powered Real Estate Investments

Blockchain is transforming the real estate market through its innate ability to streamline processes, eliminate intermediaries, and offer greater transparency. The increased accessibility provided by blockchain technology allows a much broader pool of investors to participate in the real estate market, a privilege formerly reserved for the wealthy or institutional investors. By tokenizing assets and properties, individuals can buy and sell fractions of a property, opening up new investment opportunities and contributing to a more democratic property market.

The traditional process of buying and selling real estate is fraught with inefficiencies, from lengthy property searches to time-consuming contract negotiations, not to mention costly legal fees. By leveraging smart contracts, blockchain technology removes these barriers. A smart contract is a piece of code on a blockchain network that automatically executes contractual obligations once pre-set conditions are met, thereby minimizing the need for intermediaries like solicitors and brokers.

6.2. The Mechanics of Asset Tokenization

The flexibility of blockchain enables the creation of a "token" that digitally represents a real-world asset. In terms of real estate, any property can be tokenized - residential homes, commercial properties, and even undeveloped lands. The real property is represented as a digital token on the blockchain. This token can be subdivided and traded on blockchain platforms, allowing for partial ownership of assets, and a much lower minimum investment level.

This democratizes the real estate investment landscape, as investors can purchase tokens representing fractions of a property. Tokenization of assets therefore enhances liquidity, meaning properties can now be bought and sold much more quickly and efficiently, without the need for expensive and cumbersome traditional processes.

Let's explore an example - suppose there's a commercial building worth $50 million. If this building is tokenized into 50 million tokens (each representing 0.00001% of the ownership), they can be sold to retail investors at an affordable $1 per token. This allows individuals previously unable to invest in such high-value properties to become partial owners.

6.3. Exploring Real Estate Investment Trusts (REITs) in the Blockchain Era

Real Estate Investment Trusts (REITs) are companies that own or finance real estate across a range of property sectors. Buying shares in a REIT provides a way for investors to access the lucrative property market without needing to buy the actual property. Blockchain can further enhance this model by greatly improving transparency and liquidity.

In a blockchain-powered REIT, property assets are tokenized, providing investors with the chance to buy and sell shares in the form of tokens. This approach ensures a higher level of transparency than conventional REITs, as blockchain's immutable nature makes it nearly impossible to falsify information. This provides investors with a real-time, accurate representation of the company's asset portfolio, thereby reducing the risk of fraud.

In terms of liquidity, blockchain-powered REITs offer the potential for same-day share trading settlement times, compared to the two to three-day standard set by conventional markets. This faster pace of trading opens up opportunities for more dynamic market movements, benefiting keen traders and investors.

6.4. Blockchain and Crowdfunding in Real Estate

Crowdfunding in real estate involves a group of investors pooling their funds together to buy a property. It's an effective way for small investors to participate in the property market. Blockchain technology can take this to the next level.

Imagine a platform where anyone can browse through various property listings, pick an investment that suits their budget and risk appetite, and buy property tokens. The process is swift, efficient, secure, and doesn't require extensive legal work – factors that would be possible through a blockchain-based real estate crowdfunding platform.

Moreover, by leveraging blockchain technology, the investment pool is not just restricted to national investors. It expands to a global scale, connecting property sellers and investors worldwide. Through tokenization, international investors can buy a fraction of a property without dealing with cumbersome cross-border legal procedures and hefty paperwork.

Blockchain's disruptive presence portends a new future for real estate investments. As the technology evolves and garners mainstream acceptance, blockchain could potentially unlock billions of dollars in previously hard-to-access value trapped in the world of real estate, enabling new investment opportunities for all income levels. The future of real estate investment is here, and it is brimming with possibilities.

Chapter 7. The Promise of Smart Contracts in Property Deals

Without a doubt, the most important innovation blockchain brings to property deals is the advent of smart contracts. Combining the potential of blockchain with the power of coding, smart contracts present an entirely new way to conduct real estate transactions, imparting safety, speed, precision, and financial fairness in a way that is distinct from traditional ways.

7.1. The Foundation of Smart Contracts

Smart contracts are self-executing contracts with the terms of the agreement directly written into lines of code. They exist across a distributed, decentralized blockchain network, and their information is transparent, making it visible to all participating parties. Moreover, the code controls the execution, eliminating the need for a third party.

The most noteworthy aspect of a smart contract is that it's 'smart' - not in the sense of AI sophistication, but in the scope it allocates for automation, reducing cumbersome paperwork associated with traditional property deals. Now, let's consider the major benefits and challenges of smart contracts in property deals.

7.2. Benefits of Smart Contracts in Property Deals

7.2.1. Transparency and Trust

The open-source nature of blockchain promotes transparency and fosters trust among all parties involved in a property transaction. Each transaction recorded on the blockchain is visible to all other nodes in the network. This universal visibility ensures that all parties involved in a smart contract can independently validate transactions—thereby eliminating deceptive practices and fraud.

7.2.2. Speed and Efficiency

Real estate transactions typically require lengthy verification processes involving banks, lawyers, notaries, and government bodies. Smart contracts automate these processes and significantly reduce the time to completion, sometimes to just a few minutes. This saves both time and cost on resource-intensive paperwork and verification procedures.

7.2.3. Cost Savings

Smart contracts eliminate the need for middlemen such as lawyers, notaries, and banks who typically charge a hefty fee for their services. The absence of these intermediaries results in direct and significant cost savings for property buyers and sellers.

While the benefits of smart contracts are many, it is also important to highlight that they are not necessarily a panacea. We must also investigate the potential challenges and downsides.

7.3. Challenges of Smart Contracts in Property Deals

7.3.1. Legal Recognizability

As innovation often outpaces regulation, smart contracts are not yet legally recognized or enforceable in many jurisdictions. As such, for all their potential benefits, smart contracts remain somewhat in a legal grey area, which can discourage their adoption.

7.3.2. Difficulty in Coding Legalese

Smart contracts require great precision, and even a small error or ambiguity in coding can result in dispute. As such, accurately translating the complexities of legalese into smart contract code can be a challenge without the necessary expertise.

7.3.3. Lack of a Central Authority

In a dispute, the immutability of the blockchain could potentially cause problems. Due to the absence of a centralized authority, there can be difficulties in altering a completed smart contract – even if a mistake has been made.

Despite these challenges, the overall potential for smart contracts in tackling some of the major issues in property deals is promising. As the regulatory environment evolves and blockchain technology becomes more integrated into our day-to-day lives, smart contracts are expected to gain wider adoption.

7.4. Implementing Smart Contracts in Real Estate Deals

The real challenge comes in implementing this disruptive technology in the real world. Here are a few practical steps for incorporating smart contracts into real estate transactions:

7.4.1. Employ Expertise

The first step is to employ someone with coding expertise who understands both blockchain and the complexities of law. It's a niche skill, but critical in translating the intricacies of property deals into a functioning smart contract.

7.4.2. Identify Appropriate Deal Types

Not all property deals are well-suited for smart contracts. For example, those requiring multiple verifications may still necessitate traditional methods. Start with simpler deals first, before moving into more complex ones.

7.4.3. Build a Network

A smart contract requires a distributed network to function. Creating this network can pose a challenge, but it's an integral part of setting up smart contracts. It will involve all participants (buyers, sellers, agents, and institutions), and requires openness, transparency, and trust.

In conclusion, while we are still in the early stages of smart contract implementation, their potential to revolutionize property deals is immense. The key is to embrace the change while also acclimating to new ways of conducting business. It might not be an overnight transition, but the future of real estate looks more efficient, transparent, and secure with the application of smart contracts.

Chapter 8. Overcoming Challenges with Blockchain Adoption in Real Estate

Adopting new technologies always comes with a share of challenges, and blockchain in real estate is no exception. Despite its immense potential to transform property management, operational hurdles, regulatory uncertainties, and lack of awareness create stumbling blocks in the path of its widespread adoption.

8.1. Understanding and Solving Operational Challenges

Blockchain delivers advanced functionalities, like smart contracts, property tokenization, transparent transactions, and so forth. However, integrating these into the legacy systems leads to operational complexities. Resistance to change, primarily because of the confidence in time-tested traditional methods, further complicates the matters.

Understanding how to use blockchain to generate value and simultaneously manage the transactional complexities is crucial. Implementing an effective change management strategy can play a key role here. For instance, initially, blockchain can be used for simpler tasks like record keeping, progressing gradually to more complex activities such as leasing and sales transactions. Clear communication and training will also be pivotal to explain the technological shift and create a smooth transition.

8.2. Navigating Regulatory Uncertainties

Blockchain in real estate is still in a nascent stage with unclear regulatory norms. The legal framework in various jurisdictions has yet to catch up with technology, resulting in ambiguities.

Both stakeholders and policymakers need to work collaboratively to address these issues. Policies should be designed to balance the risk with innovation. It would be beneficial to learn from areas where blockchain has been successfully applied and regulated, such as cryptocurrencies. Similarly, establishing international standards for blockchain in real estate can provide further clarity and confidence.

8.3. Addressing Lack of Awareness and Trust

Many real estate players either lack adequate knowledge about blockchain or harbor misconceptions about its usage. The presence of apparent complexities and the hype around blockchain drives this scenario.

Eradicating misconceptions and educating stakeholders in a simplistic non-technical way is vital for overcoming this hurdle. Case studies highlighting successful implementations and quantifiable benefits can help build trust. Engaging industry influencers to champion blockchain can also create a positive wave, encouraging others to follow suit.

8.4. Tackling Privacy and Security Concerns

While blockchain promotes transparency, it may inadvertently lead to privacy concerns. For example, transaction data, once added to a public blockchain, cannot be altered or removed, potentially exposing sensitive information.

Such issues can be mitigated by using a private or permissioned blockchain. In such a system, access to data can be restricted to specific parties, providing a robust control on privacy. Leveraging advanced cryptographic techniques can further ensure data security.

8.5. Overcoming Tech Limitations

Certain inherent technical limitations can hamper the scalability of blockchain. Issues like long transaction times, high energy consumption, and need for substantial storage as the transaction database grows, may limit its feasibility.

Optimizing the blockchain structure and integrating layer two solutions can address some of these limitations. Sharding, sidechains, and the introduction of energy-efficient blockchain protocols can control energy consumption and enhance scalability.

In conclusion, despite its challenges, blockchain holds the potential to revolutionize the real estate sector by overcoming the existing system's limitations. The path to blockchain's widespread adoption lies in educating stakeholders, facilitating regulatory collaborations, and innovatively solving technical limitations while ensuring security and privacy. As the technology matures and solutions to these issues become more refined, blockchain's role within real estate is set to expand, offering enhanced efficiency and creating novel opportunities for everyone in the sector.

Chapter 9. Security and Transparency: Blockchain's Dual Promise

Blockchain technology, steeped in an innovative blend of cryptography, distributed systems, and traceability, is dramatically reshaping industries, with real estate being a pivotal sector in its transformative grasp. In this context, blockchain technology promises two fundamental attributes – security and transparency – which synergistically work together to engender trust, reduce fraud, and foster a streamlined, efficient real estate ecosystem.

9.1. Blockchain: A Security Game Changer

Blockchain technology is grounded in its revolutionary approach to security through its robust decentralized system. It operates through a network of computers (nodes), each maintaining a copy of the digital ledger – the blockchain. This decentralization makes it highly resistant to fraud, hacking attempts, and data tampering, as changing any information would require a coordinated effort to alter more than half of the copies in the network, a task virtually infeasible in practice.

Each block in the blockchain contains data encrypted via cryptographic hash functions. This encryption, coupled with the fact that each block also contains the hash of the previous block, creates an inherent linkage throughout the chain. Altering a single block would, therefore, require a recalculation of that and every succeeding block's hash, an immensely resource-heavy task. This cryptography-enhanced design makes the blockchain a security force to reckon with.

For the real estate sector, which has long been plagued by problems of fraud, counterfeit documentation, and dubious transactions, blockchain's credibility and steadfast security could be instrumental in rebuilding trust and integrity within the industry.

9.2. Transparency: Blockchain's Open Ledger Paradigm

Transparency is as much a promise of the blockchain as security, achieved through its indisputable public ledger mechanism. Every transaction is recorded on the blockchain, creating a comprehensive, tamper-proof history of the asset, viewable by all participants in network.

This translates into real estate by offering a complete, immutable history of property-related transactions. If a change of ownership occurs, all parties have access to the details and history of the transaction. This level of transparency significantly reduces the likelihood of disputes and simplifies property transactions by enabling easy access to essential records.

Moreover, blockchain's transparent mechanism has the potential to streamline property due diligence processes. Presently due diligence is time-consuming and costly, mainly due to the multitude of diverse, distributed sources from which data needs to be collected, verified, and validated. Blockchain presents a unified platform where all relevant data can be accessed, drastically reducing the time and cost of due diligence, thereby influencing investment decisions in real estate.

9.3. Tokenization: Merging Security and Transparency

Tokenization is a revolutionary application of blockchain in the real estate world. By representing a real-world asset, such as property, as a digital token on the blockchain, it enables fractional ownership and democratizes investment opportunities.

The tokenized asset, backed by the security and transparency of the blockchain, carries with it every essential piece of information related to the property, from square footage and building plans to legal status and transaction history. This aligns with the principles of both security and transparency as sensitive information is protected, while only the necessary legal and transactional data is made transparently available.

Moreover, tokenization enables clearer tracking of asset ownership and transactions, which aids in preventing fraud. Tokenized assets are tough to counterfeit due to the unique digital signatures they bear, and they can't be double-sold as every transaction is instantly recorded on the blockchain.

9.4. Enhanced Trust through Smart Contracts

Smart contracts are a novel application of the blockchain that automate transactions and contracts once specific conditions are met, with the execution and enforcement happening on the blockchain. This eradicates human error, reduces fraud, and maintains transparency at the highest level.

In real estate, smart contracts could be used for various applications, including property transactions, rental agreements, or land registry transfers. Each action is contingent on the respective predefined conditions being satisfied. For example, the transfer of property ownership in a smart contract could be conditioned on the receipt of payment into a specified account.

Blockchain's security and transparency underpinning smart contracts brings an unprecedented level of trust into real estate transactions, eliminating intermediaries, and allowing parties to transact directly, securely, and transparently.

In conclusion, blockchain's dual promise of security and transparency holds the capacity to revolutionize the real estate sector, engender trust, and spur new, innovative, and inclusive forms of property management and investment. While we are only scratching the surface of blockchain's potential impacts, this nascent technology promises a transformative leap forward.

Despite the promise and potential it holds, comprehensive education and mass adoption are key to unlocking the full benefits of this technology. Hence, it is crucial that all stakeholders – developers, investors, regulators, and end-users find common ground in understanding and navigating this blockchain-enabled future of real estate.

Chapter 10. Case Studies: Successful Implementation of Blockchain in Real Estate

Traditionally, real estate transactions have been a resource-intensive process with many intermediaries, redundant records, and complex regulations. With blockchain's introduction into this conventional industry, real estate is being redefined by innovation, increasing efficiency, reducing costs, and offering enhanced security. We present two case studies to illustrate the successful implementation of blockchain in real estate.

10.1. Propy: International Property Transfers Simplified

A California-based startup, Propy, is an acclaimed example of successful blockchain implementation in the real estate sector. Propy's platform aims to redefine the home-buying process worldwide, making it more straightforward, secure, and efficient by utilizing blockchain's decentralized ledger technology.

The Propy platform allows users to view properties, make offers, carry out the transaction, and record the deed entirely within their app. Not only does this reduce the complexity of international transfers by providing exchange rates and eliminating bureaucratic paperwork, but it also makes home buying more accessible by digitizing the entire process.

Perhaps one of the most notable transactions completed through Propy was a $1.6 million property in San Francisco, bought entirely in cryptocurrency and recorded through Propy's blockchain. Ensuring the transaction was completely secure, legally compliant, and fast, Propy has shown the real potential within blockchain-based real estate.

10.2. ShelterZoom: Streamlining Real Estate Transactions

Another noteworthy success in the blockchain-real estate intersection is ShelterZoom, a company that seeks to perfect contract management, negotiation, and intermediation by leveraging blockchain technology.

ShelterZoom's platform offers real-time contract management, empowering all parties involved in a real estate transaction, including buyers, sellers, agents, and attorneys. Its transparent and interactive platform operates by storing relevant data in a secure, tamper-proof blockchain, minimizing errors, reducing processing time, and driving efficiency.

In 2018, ShelterZoom received the SIIA CODiE award for the Best Emerging Technology, affirming their success in harnessing blockchain technology's potential to streamline the real estate transaction process.

10.3. Blockchain's Impact on Land Registries

Land registries have been a particularly exciting area of blockchain application, with several countries testing and implementing blockchain systems to maintain land and property records. The Republic of Georgia, for instance, partnered with blockchain company Bitfury to develop a blockchain land-titling project.

This project not only makes land registries more transparent, immutable, and secure, but it also makes property information accessible to anyone with internet access. As a result, any form of tampering or fraud can be immediately detected and proven, a feature made possible by blockchain's immutable characteristic. By cutting out unnecessary middlemen, the process becomes much more efficient and less prone to error.

10.4. The Potential Future: Fractional Property Ownership through Tokens

Looking ahead, an exciting area expected to drive blockchain adoption in real estate is fractional property ownership. The concept of "tokenizing" assets, that is, dividing them into tradable tokens, has been a prominent discussion in blockchain technologies.

Tokenization simplifies the process of buying and selling real estate by dividing a property into smaller, more affordable units. Hence, real estate investments can be made without the need for a mortgage or large sums of capital. Such democratization could open up real estate to a broader range of investors who previously couldn't participate due to the high entry barriers.

Tokenization also provides liquidity, a traditionally challenging aspect of real estate investment. Given that tokens represent a property's share, they can be easily bought and sold on various marketplaces, bypassing the lengthy and cost-intensive traditional property selling process.

In conclusion, the implementation of blockchain in real estate has started to shake the foundations of traditional property management and transactions. As the case studies and future potential areas signify, this technology can redefine real estate as a more efficient, secure, and inclusive business. The future of blockchain in real estate is promising and is set to unlock a world of opportunities yet unknown.

Chapter 11. The Future of Blockchain in Property Management and Beyond

The dawn of the 21st century brought with it an innovation disruption wave that continues to revolutionize industries across the globe. At the forefront of this wave is blockchain technology. With its decentralized ledger system, blockchain introduces a new level of transparency, trust, and efficiency into data management and transaction handling, opening a world of possibilities for industries globally. Notable among these is the real estate sector, an industry that is ripe for an efficiency overhaul.

11.1. The Makings of a Blockchain-Powered Real Estate Industry

Blockchain, originating from the world of cryptocurrencies, is a decentralized digital ledger that records transactions across several computers, ensuring the records are tamper-resistant. Anyone in the network can see this transaction history. This transparency, combined with the immutability of records, cultivates a trust ecosystem that is independent of any central authority.

In the property management landscape, this technology translates to increased efficiency due to its ability to streamline tedious property transactions. Blockchain simplifies and accelerates the property acquisition process by reducing intermediaries, thereby cutting down on unnecessary costs and time. Furthermore, blockchain enables easy verification of property ownership, eliminating the potential for fraud.

In a blockchain-based real estate transaction, property details are uploaded to the public ledger. All transactions related to this property, such as buying, selling, and renting, can be tracked on this ledger. Moreover, buyers and sellers may transact directly, making the process more efficient and transparent than traditional real estate operations.

11.2. Blockchain and Smart Contracts: A New Appraisal System

The advent of blockchain has brought along a related technology - smart contracts. These are self-executing contracts where the terms of the agreement are written directly into lines of code. Smart contracts utilize blockchain technology to conduct and record transactions seamlessly and without human interference.

For the real estate industry, smart contracts provide a new approach to manage property agreements, including leases and rental contracts. The use of smart contracts simplifies the lease negotiation process, eliminates the need for middlemen who are traditionally involved in contract verification and ensures precise record-keeping. This reduces the overall cost of property management and increases efficiency.

If a tenant fails to pay rent by a particular date specified in the contract, the smart contract would automatically impose a penalty or notify the landlord. On the other hand, landlords can automatically renew leases, secure payments, and manage maintenance budgets, making property management easier than ever before.

11.3. Tokenization of Real Estate: A Novel Investment Opportunity

Blockchain's inherent characteristic of decentralization introduces an exciting possibility to the real estate world: tokenization.

Tokenization involves dividing property rights into tradable tokens. Each token represents a fraction of the property's ownership, and these tokens are traded on blockchain platforms.

Tokenization expands accessibility to the real estate market, allowing even small investors to participate in large property investments. With tokens, one does not need substantial capital to invest in prime real estate; instead, they can own a fraction of it. This democratization of real estate investments not only provides opportunities for small investors but attracts diverse investment portfolios, thereby leading to wealth generation and economic growth.

11.4. The Challenges Ahead

While blockchain presents numerous advantages, it's crucial to address the challenges of applying such a disruptive technology to a traditionally conservative sector.

For starters, the lack of regulatory guidelines and standardization is a significant hurdle. Ensuring the legitimacy and enforceability of blockchain transactions, particularly as they deal with assets as high-stakes as real estate, is crucial. Provisions should be made to protect participants from fraudulent actions, market manipulation, and other possible risks.

Moreover, user acceptance of blockchain technology in real estate is a challenge that needs to be overcome. It requires educating potential users about the benefits of blockchain and the security of transactions carried out through this technology.

11.5. The Road Ahead

The property management landscape, armed with the power of blockchain technology, is poised for a transformation the likes of which it has never seen before. It's no longer a question of if but how and when widespread implementation will materialize. Smart contracts, tokenization, and a seamless property transaction process point to appealing prospects for future market participants.

However, the onus is on stakeholders in the real estate and technology sectors to effectively navigate the intricate road of policy-making, regulation, and user acceptability. By forging partnerships, promoting education, and emphasizing the benefits of the technology, blockchain's integration into the real estate sector will inevitably thrive, transforming property transactions and management from their traditional models into more efficient and accessible procedures.

The ripple effects of this integration will penetrate deeper into the associated sectors, propagate increased cross-industry collaborations, and herald the shape of businesses yet to come.